Moving to Brit...

Turkey

By Cath Senker
Photography by Howard Davies

W

FRANKLIN WATTS
LONDON•SYDNEY

First published in 2008 by Franklin Watts

Franklin Watts,
338 Euston Road,
London, NW1 3BH

Franklin Watts Australia,
Level 17/207 Kent Street,
Sydney, NSW 2000

Series editor: Sarah Peutrill
Art director: Jonathan Hair
Design: Rita Storey
Photographs: Howard Davies (unless otherwise stated)

The Author and Photographer would like to thank the following with their help in the preparation of this book: Ibrahim Artic; Elif and Izmi Bozdere; Nilgun Engin, Gayhurst Community School, especially Diane Roome and Jean Whitell; Cemal, Clare, Elif, Hatice and Kömür; Hatun, Ozan and Özgen Kucukteke; Berkay, Bülent and Fatma Mustafa; Sema Firat, Hande Dogan and the children at Shoreditch Community School. We would like to thank the Mustafa family for permission to reproduce the photos on pages 12, 13, 14 and 26.

Picture credits: Steven Allan/istock photo: 10b. 4x6/istock photo: 15b. Every attempt has been made to clear copyright. Should there be any inadvertent omission please apply to the publisher for rectification.

Dewey number: 304.8'41'0561

ISBN: 978 0 7496 7860 9

Printed in China

Franklin Watts is a division of Hachette Children's Books, an Hachette Livre UK company.
www.hachettelivre.co.uk

Contents

Words in **bold** are in the glossary on page 28.

All about me

My name is Bülent Mustafa. I'm eight years old, and I'm from Turkey. I grew up in a town called Kadirli in central southern Turkey, near the coast.

Sometimes I read to my little brother Berkay.

I like playing football and other games in the park with my friends. I also enjoy swimming.

I often ride my bike near my home.

We eat Turkish meals at home. Turkish people love their food!

My family moved to Britain from Turkey three years ago. At home, we speak both English and Turkish.

My favourite Turkish dish is lahmacun (say, lahmajun). It is Turkish pizza, with mincemeat on top. I also love **kebabs**.

Meeting people

Try talking in Turkish!

Hello   *Merhaba*

What's your name?
Senim adin ne?

My name is ...   *Benim adim ....*

Where do you come from?
Hangi ülkeden geliyorsun?

I come from Turkey.
Benim ülkem Türkiye.

(Look out for more Turkish words in this book.)

Meet my family

From left to right: our close friends Elif and Izmi, me, Mum, Aunt Hatice, Grandma Elif and my brother Berkay.

I live with my mum, Fatma, and my little brother, Berkay. He's two. My dad's called Bilgin. He used to run a Turkish coffee shop, but he's not around at the moment.

My grandma and grandpa (Mum's parents) also live with us. So do two of her brothers and her sister Hatice (say 'Hateejay'). My uncle Cemal (say 'Jamal') is married to an English woman called Clare. He works in a Turkish food centre.

My mum runs the home and looks after me and Berkay. She's also studying English.

My older brother Bedri is 11, and my sister Gül is 15. They are still living in Turkey with my other grandparents.

My grandma Elif came to Britain more than 20 years ago.

Family words

Mother	*Anne*
Father	*Baba*
Sister	*Kızkardeş*
Brother	*Erkek kardeş*
Baby	*Bebek*
Grandma	*Anneanne*
Grandpa	*Babaanne*

About Turkey

Turkey lies between the Mediterranean Sea and the Black Sea. Most Turkish people are **Muslim**.

The part of Turkey west of the Bosporus is part of Europe. The eastern part lies in Asia.

Here is a map of Turkey.

A view of Ankara, the capital of Turkey.

Turkey is a very **mountainous** country. There are lowland areas near some of the coastal regions and in the south-east. Along the Black Sea coast, cherry and hazelnut trees are grown.

By the coasts, the weather is hot in the summer and warm in the winter. In the mountains, winters are very cold and snowy.

Numbers in Turkish

1	Bir
2	Iki
3	Üç
4	Dört
5	Beş
6	Altı
7	Yedi
8	Sekiz
9	Dokuz
10	On

My life in Turkey

I was born in a large city called Adana in central southern Turkey. Then we moved to Kadirli. Many people in Kadirli work as farmers growing **radishes**, **cotton** and **grain**. It is famous for its radishes. At harvest time, there's a big festival. Kadirli also has some cotton factories.

Elif, Bülent's grandma, says:

"In Turkey, it was lovely to live with the whole family together on the same street. When I first came to Britain in the 1980s, I had to leave my children behind. That was hard."

This is my uncle Imam gathering hay in my grandma's village of Tavla, about four hours' journey from Kadirli.

I went to nursery school in Turkey. In our free time, we used to go outside to play hide and seek, football and 'it'. We had orange and lemon trees in the garden, and I used to climb up to pick the fruit.

Here's a photo of me (right) when I was little in Kadirli, with my sister Gül and my brother Bedri.

This is my mum and dad in Turkey, about 14 years ago.

Moving to Britain

Our family had problems in Turkey. My dad had enemies who were making trouble for him. We needed to get away. My grandparents, two uncles and an aunt were already in Britain. It made sense to come and join them.

Bülent's Aunt Hatice says:

"I didn't like it here at first. I'm blind, and when I touched people by accident on the bus, they got upset. I couldn't explain myself. Now that I speak English well, I enjoy living here."

On the right in brown is my grandpa with some friends at a gathering in a London park many years ago.

This small park is close to my home in Hackney. My friends Özgen and Ozan are neighbours.

I was five when I arrived three years ago with my mum and dad. First we flew to Spain and then we travelled by car to Britain. We went straight to Hackney in north-east London and moved in with my grandparents.

Many Turkish people in Britain work in restaurants and food shops.

My new hometown

We live near to a big park called London Fields.

I was used to living in a town so it was not too much of a shock coming to Hackney. People from many different countries live in the area. There are African-Caribbeans and Asians as well as large numbers from Turkey and Cyprus.

Bülent's mum, Fatma, says:

"Apart from the language, it wasn't difficult to settle in London. The hardest thing about coming here was leaving behind my two older children in Turkey."

Turkish parents in Britain are **protective** of their children. In Turkey it was easier to play outside. I went out on my bike on my own even though I was only five. Here, I'm not supposed to go out alone.

Sometimes we go on school trips to central London, but I spend most of the time in my local area.

We have lots of friends and family in Hackney. Mum's cousin Ibrahim runs this local shop.

Going to school

I've got some good friends at school. Sye and I sit together at lunchtime.

When I came to Britain I started school in Year 1 at Gayhurst Community School. The school has other Turkish pupils as well as African-Caribbean, Bengali, Somali and Vietnamese children.

We have a fantastic adventure playground at school. It has a climbing frame and monkey bars.

When I started school, I didn't speak a word of English. My first teacher was called Steve. He helped me to settle in, and so did three Turkish girls in my class.

Nilgun helps me in class. I still find reading and writing English quite hard.

School in Turkey is far stricter than in Britain. No one there ever calls teachers by their first name! All schools in Turkey have a uniform.

My school day

Now I'm in Year 4, and my teacher's name is Jean. Maths is my favourite subject. Ever since I started school, I've been good at maths. I also enjoy science, especially when we do experiments. I'm not so keen on PE but I love playing outdoors at break time.

In science we made a volcano from modelling clay. We filled it with flour and **baking soda**. Jean added vinegar, and it erupted!

At Turkish after-school club we learnt how to write a simple conversation.

I go to two after-school clubs. On Mondays I learn Turkish. I can read and write a little in my language now. On Wednesdays I have help with my English. At the English club we often use computers.

Nilgun says:

"Turkish parents are very keen for their children to learn to read and write Turkish as well as English."

Free time

I enjoy playing outdoors and being active.

I spend a lot of time with my family and neighbours. I've got both Turkish and English friends nearby. We often play football behind my house or go to the park at London Fields.

Here I am practising my ball skills with Özgen and Ozan.

Mum has invited her friends for coffee and cakes. In Turkey, everyone has a coffee break at 10 a.m. Turkish people do the same here when they can.

Hobbies

Television
Televizyon

Cinema
Sinema

Computer
Bilgisayar

Football
Futbol

To relax, I like watching Turkish cartoons on a channel called Yumurcak TV. I'm a big football fan and I support the Turkish national team. Its nickname is the Ay-yıldızlar (Crescent-Stars).

Keeping our culture

On Saturdays I go to Turkish school to learn about my culture. We also keep Turkish **customs** at home. The women in my family cook delicious Turkish food.

Sheker paara (little round cakes made with semolina and a coconut topping)

Green peppers stuffed with rice

Borek (thin pastry filled with cheese or meat)

Turkish bread

Kisir (couscous with spring onions and spicy tomato sauce)

Mixed salad

Dolma (vegetable leaves stuffed with rice and meat or vegetables)

Kofta (balls of minced meat with onions and spices)

A Turkish meal.

We are Muslim, so we celebrate the **Islamic** festivals. We call them **Bayrams**. In Turkey we used to visit friends at Bayram. Here we celebrate at home.

At **Seker Bayramı** we eat sweet foods. At **Kurban Bayramı**, the Turkish community has a sheep **sacrificed**. The meat is shared out among poor people.

At the Turkish school, we wear **traditional** clothes for festivals. Men and boys wear baggy trousers and a colourful waistcoat.

My future

I am used to living in Britain now and speak English well. I would like to stay here.

I really hope that my older brother and sister can join us in London. Most of our family lives in Britain now. It would be fantastic for us all to be together.

Bülent's grandmother, Elif, says:

"I feel at home here and have never had any trouble. I like Hackney and all my neighbours are friendly, both English and Turkish. My wish is for all my family to be with me."

This photo of Gül, Bedri, Mum and me was taken before I left Turkey.

26

When I'm older, I'd like to study at **university**. My greatest aim when I grow up is to be a footballer. That would be my dream job.

Here I am playing with my Turkish friends at Saturday school. I feel at home with both Turkish and local people.

Glossary

baking soda
A white powder that is used to make cakes rise and to make fizzy drinks.

Bayram
The Turkish word for Id, a Muslim festival.

cotton
A plant grown in warm countries to make fabric.

customs
Ways of doing things.

grain
Food crop such as wheat or rice.

Islamic
Something or someone that belongs to the religion of Islam.

kebab
Small pieces of meat cooked on a wooden or metal stick.

Kurban Bayramı
The Turkish name for the Islamic festival of Id ul-Adha. Muslims remember how Ibrahim was prepared to kill his only son to show his faith in God.

mountainous
An area that has lots of mountains.

Muslim
A member of the religion of Islam.

protective
Showing a wish to protect someone from danger.

radish
A small red or white root vegetable with a strong taste.

sacrificed
An animal that is killed and given as an offering to God.

Seker Bayramı
The Turkish name for the Islamic festival of Id ul-Fitr. It is the festival that comes at the end of the Islamic month of Ramadan.

traditional
Part of the beliefs or customs of a group of people.

university
A place where many people go to study when they have left school.

Turkey fact file

Location: South-western Europe and south-western Asia, between the Mediterranean Sea and the Black Sea

Climate: Hot, dry summers and mild, wet winters

Capital city: Ankara

Population: 71 million. About four-fifths of the people are Turkish, while one-fifth are Kurdish.

Life expectancy at birth (the average age people live to): 73

Main religion: Islam

Language: Turkish. Kurdish and other languages are also spoken.

Literacy (the percentage of people over 15 who can read and write): 87%

Main jobs: Services 41%; farming 36%; industry 23%

Number of Turkish refugees: 227,000. Around 1–1.2 million Turks are internally displaced (they have had to leave their homes but are still in Turkey)

Index

Further information

All About Turkey
http://www.allaboutturkey.com/
index.htm

BBC News Country Profile: Turkey
http://news.bbc.co.uk/1/hi/
world/europe/country_profiles/
1022222.stm

Note to parents and teachers: Please note that these websites are **not** specifically for children and we strongly advise that Internet access is supervised by a responsible adult.

30